BE THE CHURCH

Beyond the Pews

AMY ROSS

BOOK PUBLISHING ASSISTANCE:

MICHELLE MORROW

WWW.CHELLREADS.COM

I dedicate this book to my grandma, who always displayed the love of Jesus in her life. She went home to be with Jesus while writing this book. I miss her every day.

CONTENTS

BE THE CHURCH

HOW WE BECAME BETHECHURCH

In her tears Mary Jane said, "Amy we have to stop playing church and BeTheChurch."

My sister in Christ, Mary Jane and I were sitting in my living room discussing the frustrations of our church experiences through the years. Mary Jane was telling me a story about her most recent encounter in the children's ministry. She had observed many of the children come from abusive homes and were inundated with trauma. It seemed no one could see them; the teachers were busy fighting about lesson plans and decorations.

One of the teachers was offended by the other for questioning her lesson plan and lack of decorating the classroom. As they yelled at each other the doors were slammed in each other's faces. Sadly, this was happening on Sunday mornings during Sunday school in front of the children. Mary Jane was devastated as she witnessed this.

Children that come to church for a glimpse of peace and safety, watch as their teachers fight and argue.

Hearing her experience caused me to express my own disappointments while in the pews. I expressed the sadness over people in the pews that came week after week full of serious problems such as Men who neglected their wife and children yet were at the church all the time working on projects. Elderly people living in hoarding situations. Teens wanting to commit suicide. No one appeared to care, I had to ask myself Why? Was it because it would take real sacrifice to disciple them or maybe they didn't pay enough in tithes to warrant the love? Could it be because they didn't belong to the right click of people? We both knew this was a common theme wherever we seemed to go.

We both started to weep as we started discussing the youth that were in sexual sin, spirit of suicide on them, the lack of understanding of the word of God even though they were raised in church. We wept for the souls not seen, the souls not tended to, the broken marriages and families that came every Sunday and even served and yet no one knew the truth of what was going on behind closed doors. Not even the church leaders took the time to really get to know those they are supposedly overseeing. It was a church of maybe forty people yet seemed no one had time for discipleship.

Several things had happened on this particular week to several people/families that caused us to be particularly anguished. These saints had been going through these things for years and yet no one in leadership cared or even tried to help.

We are going to BeTheChurch!

She was disappointed not only in "leadership" but in the body of Christ at this ministry as well. It is not just "leaderships" responsibility to tend to souls. We are all called to encourage, disciple, love, hold each other accountable; to be a family of God. Mary Jane made this hashtag sign with her fingers as she said, "Amy we have to stop playing church and start BeingTheChurch!"

INTRODUCTION

I want to say I LOVE the church of God. I want you to know that before I tell my story. I love His bride so much it hurts my heart to see current happenings in the church.

I know there are great ministries out there trying so hard to be the church. I know many great men and women of God who are trying to walk in unity and love. There are great pastors who have dedicated their entire lives to the study of God's word and the washing of the feet of Gods people.

This book and my own personal experiences are not meant to be a gunshot fired at each and every ministry. However, I believe we can all do better. None of us have arrived at perfection. If something you read jolts you praise God, ask Him for help to change. If you read this entire book and have no conviction, then let it go.

I pray you are not part of the problem and have chosen to ignore the problem that seems to be staring directly into our faces.

Again, I want to reiterate how much I love the body of Christ. However, I am struggling to tolerate the lukewarm complacent unloving worldly "church."

God is still working on me in grace. I have come a long way in this area. I used to be pretty zealous and would just whip out a sword with truth without a whole lot of love. I pray a lot before I speak now. There is so much I want to say, and Holy Spirit has taught me temperance.

THE LORD NUDGES

We felt the Lord wanted us to take what we did with home bible studies, inner healing and deliverance, discipleship, outreaches, etc. and become more public with it. We were looking at changing the name of our old ministry and rebranding. We had been doing all these things for many years, but no one really knew about it unless you knew us personally. We felt the Lord nudging us to become more of a ministry that is known instead of just being so silent about things. Not because we need to be seen but because **He is to be made known**. I believe He had been training us through those years in the small things and was now ready to give us more.

With the rise of social media and a desire to reach more people for Christ we too wanted to take the ministry more public. The name we had wasn't really catchy—Bride without Spot and Blemish. We had a Facebook page but didn't maximize the use of it. We taught bible studies in the home, but it was only a few of us. BeTheChurch says it all and so we changed our ministry name to what we felt encompasses everything we wanted to be about.

BETHECHURCH COMES ALIVE

I got to work immediately and changed the name of our discussion page. I setup a new business non-profit page, Instagram, twitter, and YouTube. God showed me the logo colors, black background with white lettering. The black represents the darkness of sin in the world and the white represents the light of Christ exposing the darkness and his children being the light that represents Christ in this dark world.

We reached out to our community and invited more people to bible study. We made t-shirts that would be conversation starters. We had flyers made to pass out as we talked to people about Jesus. We started putting our outreaches on public forums, again not for people to see us but to show people anyone can go reach the lost or help the hurting. We knew that we didn't have to be a big group, have to have a lot of money, or have to have a degree in theology to **Be The Church**.

We are obedient to God and He has blessed the ministry. We are now into our fourth year since changing the name and rebranding. We have a family of believers that are catching the same vision and are going beyond the pews to **BeTheChurch**.

FALSE CONVERT

My grandmother, a God-fearing woman, loved Jesus so much that she would talk to me about Him every chance she could. I watched her bend her knees every night praying to Him before she crawled into bed. I then witnessed her every morning getting out of bed and immediately bending her knee again before starting her day. She would make a fresh cup of coffee and sit at the kitchen table and read her bible. It was her faithful routine every day of her life. No matter what trials came her way she would say, "I know Jesus will work it out."

She would say to me, "Amy no matter what have faith in Jesus and read your bible." And "Amy you have to know the bible for yourself."

As a young child I didn't fully understand but I sure

did love my grandma and so I wanted whatever she had. I was abused as a child, so my grandma's house was my escape. She always made me feel loved and wanted. Grandma would speak life over me and encourage me. She represented Jesus to me which is a key to our Christian walk. She was not only telling me about Jesus, but she represented Him to me in her own life.

The first time I remember asking Jesus into my heart was with my grandma. We were in her car getting ready to go somewhere and she had on her Christian radio program. The preacher proclaimed, "If you want to go to heaven then just ask Jesus into your heart right now."

Of course, I was five years old and certainly wanted to go to heaven. I wanted the Jesus my grandmother was always talking about. I looked over at my grandma with my big brown five-year-old eyes and said, "Grandma I want to go to heaven, and I want Jesus to come into my heart"!

She was so excited as any good Christian grandmother is. She had me repeat a prayer with her asking Jesus into my heart. That was it. I was told I was now a Christian. I had no idea what that meant but I was glad to make my grandma so proud of me and heaven sounded nice too.

Neither one of my parents knew Christ. The only time I was able to go to church was with my grandma. As a child I loved church. I would go to Sunday school and try so hard to earn the stars for attendance. The most I ever got was two stars because I never made it more than two weeks in a row. It would leave me feeling sad and rejected. You had to come at least three weeks in a row to get the third shiny star that earned you a prize from the toy chest. I desired to be there, but it was out of my control as a child.

My only safe place was at my grandma's.

I was living in an abusive home environment and my dad was not around much for various reasons. I am a survivor of molestation and sexual abuse which caused me a lot of trauma and pain in my childhood. I never felt good enough or wanted, other than for men's sexual pleasure.

I grew up to become a rebellious teenager. I only believed I was worth something sexually. This caused me to become sexually active at a young age. I had no boundaries with sexual activity. I wanted to only please my boyfriend in order to keep him interested as I had a fear of abandonment created out of my dad being an absentee father. I remember feeling guilty for being sexually active because I knew in my heart it was wrong. I would go home at night and tell Jesus I was sorry, but I would go out the next day and do it again. I loved my sin; I just didn't want to go to hell because of it. My sin only grew within me as I kept getting older. Sex, pot smoking, drinking, night clubs, desiring success, and money. I was the girl that would do debates about Jesus while drinking a beer. I would be out all night at the bar on Saturday but in church on Sunday.

I worshipped God with my mouth, but my heart was far from Him.

I had also become intrigued with occult practices. It started out with what seemed innocent, like horoscopes and astrology. I played with a Ouija board a couple times. Me and my friends would play light as a feather stiff as a board every time we had a sleep over. We did seances and whatever else seemed spooky at the time. This made me feel like I had some sort of control of this universe that had controlled me for so long. By the time I was 18 I had opened many doors to the occult including a spell that gave my soul to satan.

The night I did that spell a large black evil figure woke me up in the middle of the night. This demonic spirit was hovering almost nose to nose to me. I could feel the evil. I knew it wanted to kill me. It is hard to explain but hatred, evil, murder everything vile is all I could feel emanating off this creature of hell. I instantly cried out to Jesus and repented. The black figure left my room immediately. However, I had serious repercussions from that night. Between this experience and the doors, I had opened with my sinful nature it took years before I became truly delivered and set free. Messing with the occult is no game, as I would discover over the next 15 years.

I begged Jesus to come back into my heart and forgive me.

By the time I was 21 I had a baby out of wedlock living with my boyfriend. I ended up with PTSD, Acute Panic Attacks, Agoraphobia (hard to leave the house due to fear of something bad happening to you), and depression which led to suicidal thoughts. Between my sin, the occult practices, and my childhood I was a mess in every way.

I remember my grandma would always say, "No matter what Amy seek Jesus; He is the only answer to any problem."

I wanted to be free so badly that I started seeking Jesus every day. I would read my bible because that is what grandma did.

I would pray because that's what grandma did. I would listen to TV preachers because that's what grandma did.

I even married my live-in boyfriend because Grandma said it was a sin to live with someone outside of marriage. I was willing to do anything to bargain with God for my healing.

I would feel somewhat better because the teachers I listened to were very pop culture, feel good, best life humanism type teaching.

I wanted to be free from PTSD, Panic Attacks and every other chain that bound me.

They were motivational speakers in the Name of Jesus. I was maturing as a human because they gave good moral advice, but I was not maturing in Christ nor was I changing on the inside. I honestly still did not want the Jesus of the bible. I didn't want to carry a cross or deny my flesh. I was young and wanted to be out enjoying life with my friends. I just didn't want to be in this hell in my head that had trapped me inside my home most days. I had great ambition, but fear held me back in the worst way.

Sadly, every pastor, leader, and Christian I encountered also justified it with me.

I eventually left my first husband and started dating another man who is now my current husband of 22 years. I was once again in sexual sin, at the bars and still in church on Sundays. I justified it *all*. My first pastor baptized me in water knowing I was living with my boyfriend; then he dedicated my baby before God knowing also, I was living with my boyfriend. My other pastor said he didn't have any problem with me living with my boyfriend and I could become a member of the church. I was seriously lost in a religious system of Christianity but no real relationship with Jesus or freedom in my life.

My emotional state got worse after years of trying to be the perfect mom, perfect coach, perfect wife, perfect stepmom, perfect friend, daughter, Christian, etc.

I finally broke.

I could barely function, I couldn't eat and become absolutely exhausted in every way. I developed Chronic Fatigue Disorder and started to have suicidal thoughts again. I was miserable.

I kept fighting for a relationship with Jesus. I kept believing He was the answer to my problems. I was still incredibly involved with humanism or moral Christianity. Humanism means giving man made solutions to spiritual problems. We use the bible to make our lives here on earth better in a moralistic way. A good example is "10 keys to your best life now" or "15 ways to have a better marriage" or "20 ways to become wealthy God's way". Sadly, none of this was working in my life for the deep spiritual emotional issues I had.

I would cry every day for God to heal me.

I would go to every alter call. I would call prayer hot lines. I always said I was the healthiest sick person on the planet because I was physically healthy, but I was so bound up emotionally that I couldn't function. I found myself on Xanax and other anxiety drugs to cope. However, that only worked for a short season before the drugs turned on me and were no longer effective. I was trying every man-made solution for a spiritual problem.

My husband and I become the head of a church by default, long story for another time. Here we are with this church in our lap to now run. My husband had no desire to pastor a church at that time, I was a hot mess emotionally. So, we hired a pastor and grew this church from 8 people to on average 100 people within 4-6 months. I went from youth leader to head of women's ministry. My husband was the CFO and head deacon on our board. We had no elders only the pastor and deacon board. I went from having my own emotional issues to now a room full of women who all needed me and were mostly new converts too. Looking back, I think we were all imparting demons to each other. We had false prophets running around, women seeing visions, people who were demon possessed, pharisees and so much more. I could write a book just on some of the experiences from this church alone, and maybe one day I will.

After about one and a half years into running this ministry, I finally had enough. I was being tortured by the enemy; God seemed nowhere to be found. I was dealing with PTSD, Panic Attacks, depression, suicidal thoughts and now physically I had Chronic Fatigue Syndrome. Demons were manifesting in my bedroom and causing all kinds of issues. I was someone who was aware demons existed but not a believer in constant attacks and seeing them manifest. I had no business being the head of an ant farm more or less a ministry of Gods people. However, my pride was too big to admit I was not mature enough to handle it. I used the same humanism I was taught all those years. However, there is no power in humanism and satan took full advantage of my ignorance.

> *I had made a promise to God that if He healed me,*
> *I would serve Him all the days of my life.*

I genuinely loved the people and I thought if I served Christ with all I had He would be proud of me and finally heal me. Maybe I could work my way into God's favor, so I thought. However, I was still sold out to the prosperity gospel and culture Christianity. Was I really ready to serve Christ with everything I had?

The answer at the time was **NO!**

One day my husband was outside working, and I was on the porch watching him. I felt sorry for myself because I had no energy at all to try and help him. All the sudden I heard a voice that said, "Amy how do you know Christ is the answer?"

I turned my head and exclaimed, "What?"

The voice said, "You have been like this for thirteen years now, you cry out to God, you do all these things for God, yet He hasn't healed you. If anything, you have only gotten worse. How do you know that Jesus is the right way, how do you know for sure it's not Muhammad, Krishna, Buddha, or something else, have you even tried another religion to see if you are following the true God?"

The devil was basically asking me, "Where is your God? Where do you see Him in your life?"

Gripped by fear, I went inside my house. For the first time ever, I questioned if God was real.

Is Jesus real?

Is Jesus the only way?

I have to go find Jesus.

I faced the reality that maybe I only followed Jesus because my grandma did. It did seem as if God didn't care or wasn't hearing my cries all these years. However, everything in my inner being knew Jesus was the only way. I doubted only for a few seconds before I got mad at the voice of doubt and deception. How dare satan try to talk to me and make me doubt my God. I did have to face the reality though that I wasn't seeing the Jesus of scripture in my life.

I was not free.

I didn't see Jesus in my church or anywhere else for that matter. We all talked about Him, but did we really abide in Him?

Were we transformed?

Was I a new creation?

I called my pastor and my assistant and said, "I will not be back for forty days." I know they thought I was crazy, but the truth was, I was crazy and that's why I needed to find Jesus. I felt like the women with the flow of blood that no one could figure out why she wouldn't stop bleeding. I was bound and determined to find Jesus and touch the hem of His garment once and for all and nobody was going to stop me.

I NEVER KNEW YOU

MY SALVATION EXPERIENCE

I never experienced the Jesus of scripture.

*T*truly had not seen the Power of Jesus in my life. I certainly did not see His love or power in the churches I attended. I kept fighting in my own strength and it was wearing me out. I was that same girl who did speeches on Jesus in front of my peers but had no transformed life of my own. Nothing had changed. I was a right fighter, a debater, very opinionated and I believed Jesus was real because my grandma was real to me. She was my faith. She was my Jesus in many ways.

I also had several dreams as a teenager about Jesus.

One dream He came to me and told me I was going down the wrong road. He warned me of Hell, He seemed to be drawing me to Him. There was something deep inside of me that said Jesus is the answer, He is real, you just need to go find Him.

I wanted the Jesus of scripture.

That day on my porch I told God I was going to lay down everything I had ever been taught about Christianity, Jesus, Church, Religion etc. and I was going to go find Jesus. I wanted the real Jesus. All of the sudden this peace came over me and I felt God press upon my heart as if to say, "Thank you, I wish more of my children would come find the true Me."

That was it. I was on a journey. I got a note pad and I just sought Jesus. The next forty days I went to several different churches. I read my bible every day seeking God for answers. I prayed, fasted, cried, and just felt so free to search for Jesus. The journey became a season of years of searching not just forty days.

One day in my bedroom I was reading the bible. I came across a familiar passage:

> "Not everyone who says to me, 'Lord, Lord,' will enter the kingdom of heaven, but the one who does the will of my Father who is in heaven. On that day many will say to me, 'Lord, Lord, did we not prophesy in your name, and cast out demons in your name, and do many mighty works in your name?' And then will I declare to them, 'I never knew you; depart from me, you workers of lawlessness.'"
>
> — *MATTHEW 7:21-23*

The Spirit of the Lord came on me so strong.

He said, "That is you, Amy."

I said, "What, Huh, me Lord? What are You saying?"

He said, "Amy if you were to die this would be you!"

I argued with the Lord for a second.

"How is that possible Lord? I was the head of woman's ministry, I read your bible, I evangelize to people, I tell everyone I am a Christian."

He said, "I will say, AMY, I never knew you!"

It hit me so hard because I realized I did the same

thing. I gave Him all the reasons why I am saved but He said I never knew you in the passage.

I was wrestling with God.

I was still in disbelief because I don't understand how I couldn't be saved because I knew in my heart of hearts that I love Jesus. Or so I thought I did. I started frantically just flipping through pages of my bible I was in total disbelief. All the sudden my bible landed to:

"and with all wicked deception for those who are perishing because they refused to love the truth and so be saved. Therefore, God sends them a strong delusion, so that they may believe what is false, in order that all may be condemned who did not believe the truth but had pleasure in unrighteousness."

— *2 THESSALONIANS 2:10-11*

The Spirit revealed to me that I had refused to believe the truth about sin, holiness, God's plan of salvation and what it means to be truly born again. So, God put me under a strong delusion to think I was saved, when in fact I wasn't.

My heart sank to my stomach, I felt like I was going

to throw up. I continued to cry out to God in disbelief and kept thumbing through the bible frantically. I turned to:

"Everyone who makes a practice of sinning also practices lawlessness; sin is lawlessness. You know that he appeared in order to take away sins, and in him there is no sin. No one who abides in him keeps on sinning; no one who keeps on sinning has either seen him or known him. Little children let no one deceive you. Whoever practices righteousness is righteous, as he is righteous. Whoever makes a practice of sinning is of the devil, for the devil has been sinning from the beginning. The reason the Son of God appeared was to destroy the works of the devil. No one born of God makes a practice of sinning, for God's seed abides in him; and he cannot keep on sinning, because he has been born of God. By this it is evident who are the children of God, and who are the children of the devil: whoever does not practice righteousness is not of God, nor is the one who does not love his brother."

— 1 JOHN 3:4-10

I said, "God if I am not saved then who is?"

Because by my works inside a church building it would have appeared, I was a Christian.

He took me back to Matthew 7: 13-20.

"Enter by the narrow gate. For the gate is wide and the way is easy that leads to destruction, and those who enter by it are many. For the gate is narrow and the way is hard that leads to life, and those who find it are few. Beware of false prophets, who come to you in sheep's clothing but inwardly are ravenous wolves. You will recognize them by their fruits. Are grapes gathered from thorn bushes, or figs from thistles? So, every healthy tree bears good fruit, but the diseased tree bears bad fruit. A healthy tree cannot bear bad fruit, nor can a diseased tree bear good fruit. Every tree that does not bear good fruit is cut down and thrown into the fire. Thus, you will recognize them by their fruits."

I repented of all my sin and begged Him for mercy on my soul.

I knew at that moment I was not saved. I jumped out of my bed and laid flat on my face on the floor of my bedroom. I was weeping hysterically and crying out for God to save me. I repented for not believing His word about sin and holiness. I repented for buying into false gospels of health, wealth, and prosperity. I repented for witchcraft in my past. I just kept repenting for everything Holy Spirit brought to my remembrance. I laid on my floor for probably two hours. I don't know if God saved me at that very moment, but I do know I become transformed in that season.

Shortly after my encounter with God in my bedroom I got delivered from demons of witchcraft. I know because I became a brand-new creation in Christ. I was set free from PTSD, Panic Attacks, Depression, Suicidal Thoughts, Chronic Fatigue Syndrome, Co-Dependency, love of money, materialism, sexual immorality through porn and lust and so much more.

God had my husband and I walk away from the ministry we birthed out. The pastor was in sin and God said, "Walk away." God shut the church down five months later. We were hurt deeply in that ministry because we did not defend ourselves, God made us keep our mouths shut and simply walk away.

All these years later we have been vindicated by God. Truth of the leader's sexual sin came out exposing them as false converts. Many of them have walked away from the faith sadly. We learned so much in those painful years.

The real Jesus is the **Jesus of Scripture**. He is a

loving God. **He is a Holy God.** There is evidence of our salvation. That evidence is marked by a life of holiness. We are not perfect, but we do not go on habitually willfully sinning against God. When we meet Jesus, everything changes. We become born again. We really do have a born-again experience. This is a supernatural God given experience that cannot be fully understood by someone who has never had it.

The living God, Creator of the Universe touches you with His supernatural regenerating power of His Spirit. All the shed blood of Jesus is applied to your account of sin.

Suddenly your eyes are opened, the scales fall off and you can see things so clearly now. I understand the deep things of God now. I not only understand His word, but I love His word. I love theology and doctrine. I love my brothers and sisters. I have a burning passion for the lost. I love being with the least of these. I no longer want success and money. I don't need to be seen nor do I desire positions and titles. I only want Christ alone known to the world. I want the real Jesus to be seen and realized in everyone's life.

I am completely transformed.

THE JOURNEY

*A*fter leaving the ministry we birthed, I found myself in this church in the middle of my neighboring city. This church had a woman apostle named Yvonne. Yvonne was so charismatic and knew how to build people up. Yvonne had people surrounding her who did her bidding all day. One lady named Kathy would run errands day and night for her, clean her house, do her grocery shopping. Kathy was not paid for this service but rather was taught this what you do for "leaders" of God. She would work a long shift and then run around franticly trying to please her "master."

It was actually painful to watch Kathy, who had low self-esteem and trauma, lose herself to the abuse of trying to gain approval from Yvonne. Yvonne had several around her that did whatever she said. She taught us that it was our job to serve her and obey her because she is God's anointed Apostle over us.

After experiencing such a loss from the other ministry, I was searching still for the real Jesus and inner healing. I was broken. I was attracted to her strength as a woman I wanted to be whole and strong like Yvonne. However, I realized her strength was not one I wanted after all considering it was manipulation and control.

She knew how to minister to people to get them to need her. I was hurting and I needed someone to help me figure all this out. God placed me with her for a few months. However, as I started to listen to her teach, I understood she was teaching false theology.

Yvonne taught that Jesus was not God. She taught satan created the dinosaurs. She taught as a Christian if you sin even one second before you die you would be in hell. I actively praise God for the Holy Spirit who will guide you into all truth because everything in me knew what this woman was teaching was false.

At the time I was coming out of the "word of faith" movement which caused me to not know true Christian Theology. I was ignorant to foundational orthodox Christian truths the bible taught. However, Holy Spirit knew.

God would make me go home after her teachings

and study for hours on each topic. This was before the great influence of searching the internet or watching YouTube. I had to grab my bible and study with the Holy Spirit and a few commentaries I just happened to have on hand.

What satan means for evil God will turn around for His glory and our good if we love Him.

After several months of Yvonne's false teachings, I finally left her ministry. God can use a donkey and though she was a false teacher I did learn things I needed to learn. It was in her ministry I realized demons are real. I started to understand we are at war in the spiritual realm. I learned to search out my word for every question I had. He knew I was on a journey, so He allowed me to experience some things good from that ministry. He also had me learn truth by being in a false church.

I had a study room dedicated to God. I spent hours in my study each day reading the bible, worshipping, and praying. When I left her ministry that week my entire study was plagued with bees. We have never had a bee problem. We could not find a nest anywhere outside or inside. The bees were only in that room, and they were everywhere. Overnight I had hundreds of bees. They were dead and alive. I didn't think too much of it because I was pretty naive to this kind of thing happening in real life.

However, one day I talked to another lady, Jean, who had left the ministry before I did, and she happened to mention that right after she left her entire house was full of gnats. She never had an issue with gnats before other than the occasional fruit gnats that might come in from the market. She said her whole house was full of them. She knew however that it was from Yvonne's ministry. Jean brought in a prayer team to pray over her home. After they prayed the gnats died and went away.

It was only then I realized the bees were witchcraft and not some freak of nature. I remember having dreams all the time about Yvonne and in my dreams, she was calling me back to her ministry. The dreams would have her telling me I need her, and I must return to her. In those dreams it would have her saying, "You can't be healed without me. You have to come back to me to find God," and other things like that. And it carried on to the point that after six months I went back just for one Sunday and asked Yvonne to release me from her ministry. At the time I didn't realize it was witchcraft plaguing me, I assumed it my guilty conscience for leaving. The dreams stopped and I eventually got away from her pull. Still to this day I have never met anyone like her in ministry.

My journey began again to find Jesus. At this point I was in my word all the time. I was in my study probably four to six hours a day Monday through Friday while my daughter was in school.

My search for Jesus became my part time job.

As I was trying to find a new home church, I would attend different ministries and within weeks or only a couple months things would just surface. One thing that was a common theme in all of these churches was the winking at sexual sin. People in sexual sin while serving in all types of capacity in the church. Worship leaders preying on vulnerable women in the congregations. I witnessed Pastors having affairs outside their marriages. Sexual sin abounded everywhere I went. Meanwhile, I was reading my bible and studying it like never before and I could not believe how far the church had come from what I was reading.

My heart would ache as I saw the disregard for God's word. The leaders and members would justify sexual sin, drinking, gluttony, gossip, lying, stealing, anger outburst, jealousies, contentions, and divorce. It seemed all we cared about was money to keep the buildings going. So, we needed to fluff up our messages, so the chairs stayed full.

WHAT HAPPENED TO OUR CHURCHES?

Our churches had become social clubs. Is that what we were meant to be? Are we just a place to gather once or twice a week? Since I show up to church then it justifies my rebellion the rest of the week? Is it just a good moral place to take our children? Is it a healthy place to raise a family? Is it just what we do in America, we go to church? My grandparents always went, so we should go. We feel better knowing we are church goers. We found a place that appreciates us. I fit in more here, I am needed. Its free entertainment? Are these the things we tell ourselves?

> *I wept during service thinking,*
> *"Jesus where are You in these buildings?"*

The more I searched the more frustrated I became with what I was seeing. It wasn't just the sexual sin that had me so heartbroken, but it was the lack of love. I remember that one time in the first couple weeks of my journey I was so emotionally exhausted I had an argument with my husband. That argument made me feel like I wanted to die. The spirit of suicide was still speaking to me. I attended a local church by myself for the first time and not one person spoke to me. I had to fill out a visitor card and had a question about it so I asked one of the deacons/ushers something and he was so rude to me I couldn't believe it. I never felt so alone in a room full of "Christians" in my life. I left feeling even more defeated than when I showed up.

The journey took me to different states and even internationally. One time we were in North Carolina with some famous "Christian" people. We would go up to a beautiful cabin in the mountains with a few others. We spent the weekend with these people on multiple occasions. God connected us to them for a season. On one occasion the "apostle" or "prophet" over the entire movement, Bob Jones was with us for the weekend. He was known worldwide and I was excited to spend the weekend with him. There was only a few of us in this cabin together so we became quite close.

The famous "prophet" brought his family with him. His wife and adult children whom I presume he was grooming to take over his ministry. I noticed he never worshipped with us. We were a small group in a living room type setting and him and his family would just sit there waiting for their time to speak to us. We would be in powerful worship. On our faces weeping and crying, singing to Jesus for long periods of time. Him nor his wife or adult children moved. They didn't raise their hands or have any emotion at all, they had these dead stares. They sat there cold faced just waiting for the microphone. I am not saying worship is an emotion but for all four of them to be stone faced and not actively worshipping at all? I remember praying to God and saying, "Lord never let me get so famous or so popular or so prideful that I stop worshipping you."

I was so taken back by it that everything he taught was meaningless to me. I wrote all his prophecies down in a journal and none of it came to pass. I have no idea how he became the head of that movement because I didn't see a man after God's own heart or an accurate prophet before me. I saw a well-rehearsed public speaker.

In that same weekend I remember him telling everyone it was time to go to heaven and he snapped his fingers and immediately as if on cue everyone who attended the weekend retreat went into hysterical laughter and fell on the floor. There was only a handful of us that just looked at each other with disbelief.

While most of the people were hysterically laughing on the floor a man came running in with feathers claiming he found them in his room. Feathers in this movement represents angelic visitations. I was trying to be open to all things God, as I was on a journey to find Him, after all. I needed to remain teachable and open to whatever God wanted to show me. However, I had this overwhelming feeling come over me and I knew I had to get out of the living room.

I went to my bedroom and laid on the floor and wept like a baby. I felt demonic spirits surrounding me and could hardly breath. I cried out to God for help and begged Him for mercy as I believe we had opened ourselves up to ungodly spirits that weekend. I knew something was very wrong and I wanted to leave.

That was the last time we went and hung out with the leaders in that movement again. I knew we had to cut ties and go back to our search for Jesus.

God knew my heart in serving Him and wanting truth.

I learned a lot about Jesus during that time. I did learn that He is more than a religion. He really is a relationship. A personal radical love relationship. God allowed us to experience amazing things during this season. I saw miraculous healings, walked in many signs and wonders, grew in many of my spiritual gifts. However, I also saw the dark side of that movement. I saw the demons that ran amuck. The theology was becoming extremely poor, and the new age movement was starting to creep in more and more. He used that time to show me His truth within the lies. satan always has some truth in his lies of deception. This is why we must know the bible for ourselves and be able to rightly divide it. The devil is crafty in his deceptions and twists God's word to cause untrained saints to fall into his traps.

The more I read my word the more the teachings were not lining up with who God really is, who Jesus is and what true salvation is. Again, God allowed me to be on that journey for a season. I believe because I can now warn people about it but also, He used it to teach me a beautiful side of my salvation I may have never known otherwise. Something else I learned is my brothers and sisters are in that movement. I do not endorse the teachers, but I have some wonderful brothers and sisters that love Jesus and have given their lives to Him. I have missionary friends from that movement that sold everything and moved to Brazil. They are not heavy in the movement anymore; God draws His people out eventually from false religions or churches if they are truly seeking Him. However, we must be aware that our brothers and sisters are in all kinds of places that are not orthodox or even considered Christian. They need to be shown the truth so the truth can set them free. Many are just unaware because they are not discipled through the word.

After leaving that NAR known as the New Apostolic Reformation and Vineyard Movement, I was surely closer to finding Jesus. I became even more passionate about God's word. I couldn't get enough of His word and I wanted to be equipped. By this time, I wanted to be in full time ministry. I was ready to sell everything we had and serve Jesus with all I am.

When I started job hunting in full time ministry most churches wanted their staff to have a bachelor's degree. I love the bible and I love to study so I did what every good Christian who wants to be in full time ministry does, went to college.

I am not knocking formal education at all. I am saying *this is not* what qualified us for the work of the Lord as you will read.

The bible college we chose was in West Virginia but had campuses in Southern Ohio. It was accredited and affordable at the time since my husband and I both wanted to attend at the same time to attain our degrees. We purchased a year-round camping site with a trailer on it in southern Ohio just so we could go to college during the week and then be home on the weekends.

Often times we had to take classes in West Virginia because the classes were not offered in Southern Ohio.

We would drive the one and half hours each way to school several days a week. We took as many classes each semester as we could so we could accelerate graduation.

I do not really remember where we were going to church at the time. I feel like Bible College was our church back then. We basically ate slept and breathed college. My husband ended up with his pastoral degree and I received my degree in divinity with a minor in missions.

While we were in college, we met a lady who told us about her uncle and aunt that moved to Honduras and started a ministry there. We were praying at the time to go on a mission's trip. I really believed that Jesus was not really in America, and that I could find Him in the persecuted areas of the world.

We ended up getting their information and long story short we ended up in Honduras over Holiday break from college. We were about to graduate college and were ready for our next journey of full-time ministry. They were looking for a couple to help take over their ministry as they were getting older and wanted to spend more time in the states. We loved Honduras but God said no to the mission field. Our daughter just left for college at the time and wanted to return home and go to a local university. We both didn't feel the call there in Honduras but still wanted to serve Christ full time.

We had spent thirteen years now going through all the hoops of man to try and find Jesus. We attended every marriage conference there was for the first eight years of our marriage we traveled all over the Nation getting equipped in biblical marriage: Weekend to Remember, Love Languages, DNA of Marriage, Catholic Weekend Marriage Retreat and many more.

We took financial classes to learn how to teach biblical finance. I took deliverance and inner healing classes from three different schools. Took prophetic classes, evangelism classes. I got my nouthetic counseling degree (this is a method of counseling that uses only scripture). We took leadership classes and bible theology classes. When I say we jumped through hoop after hoop I am not kidding. We even started to take classes on how to minister to abortion minded women. Finally, in the middle of that class and the end of our bachelor's degrees is when we felt God press upon our hearts STOP! Stop looking to every man-made program and book and class. Stop jumping through every hoop man puts in front of you.

He wanted us in our bibles and seeking His face.

I believe it was time for God to equip us.

We had done it the "Christian" worlds way for so long that we burnt out. We really thought the more degrees and certificates we had the more qualified we would become to someone. We thought we could apply for a Pastoral Position or Apply for a leadership position in a Christian organization and get the job with our credentials. We just wanted to work for the Lord. At the time we thought that meant Position, Title because we have to still pay bills after all.

We sold our House, business, cars and more. We downsized into a much smaller home. We went to work regular jobs and ended up in a reformed church in North Canton Ohio. We wanted to live a simpler humbler life. We wanted to figure out where God would have us to be. My husband received amazing discipleship by the men there.

I know that this season was for my husband. We were there three years. In that three years, I watched my husband blossom into the man he was called to be even though I found myself in a dry season. I had been jumping through hoops to learn more and more. I had always been teaching some sort of bible study or class or was the head of a ministry such as kids, teens, women's etc.

I felt lost during this season.

It was hard for me to sit still. However, I know this

time was for my husband's training under solid biblical men. I did begin to feel like God wasn't going to use us. I thought maybe all those prophecies spoken over us were wrong. Maybe the dreams I had were emotional. Maybe all the things I felt God show me was just my vain imagination. I started to get discouraged which did make me get complacent and lukewarm with my walk for a short season.

I loved my reformed brothers and sisters so much, but I never felt comfortable there. I was so passionate about worship, and I love the gifts of the Holy Spirit. Sometimes I just needed to weep at the alter but there was no alter. Sometimes I wanted to shout to the Lord in worship but that's not accepted there. The word was preached so beautifully. They had good discipleship for the men. It was a great ministry, but we moved out of the area after our daughter graduated college.

So, it was a new season once again.

God gave me a new fire for ministry.

We wanted to move back to our hometown to be closer to our family and friends again. We found a church right down the road. We thought it would be perfect. They preached holiness and had good worship music. It was a small church and it felt more intimate.

After three years of being at our reformed church just sitting in the pews, I was ready to go full force again. This time we both had no desire for titles or positions. We honestly fell in love with Acts chapter two's idea of church. We really felt that God was calling us to love people and make Christ known.

We had a home bible study like we have had throughout the years. We evangelized and fed the homeless, worked in inner healing and deliverance. We had a cute little name for it "Bride without spot and blemish ministry." It was not a public ministry we used the name for a Facebook group and when we served people wanted to have a name of a ministry. However, my heart for "leadership" or "position" changed. We no longer wanted anything to do with things that would prop us up.

I gave that little church all of me. I cooked meals, loved people, taught bible studies, home visits, nursing home visits. I helped at every function and ministered to people. I honestly didn't want anything from them. I really wanted to serve. God had developed in us a desire for people not the pulpit. Leaders lead by example.

We didn't need a title to love people.

We didn't need a title to teach people His word.

We didn't' need a title to hit the streets.

We needed Jesus!

The world had made us feel that we needed to have titles and positions in order to make money to provide for our basic needs so that we could serve people full-time. That's all we knew; we had only seen that model in all our church experience. God gave us a different model, a biblical model. A model of being the church.

We were trying to really settle into the neighborhood church we were now attending as we held home bible studies and did outreaches, we thought we could encourage people to come to our church and grow the small congregation.

We were noticing though that love was given to certain people, but others were shunned. We experienced gossip and rudeness on a whole new level. People were coming to church but not being noticed of the need for help with sin and brokenness in their lives. We started to see a very legalistic religious spirit rooted in the people. It was all about preaching holiness but living like pharisees and not really being there for each other in need.

The gossip inside church astounds me. I seriously do not think anyone goes one on one anymore. We have created a culture that can talk about anyone for any reason, and no one is willing to put a stop to it. We think "leaders" are above the scripture, so it's ok to go to them before going to our brother or sister. We think it is ok to talk to everyone else before getting all the facts because we run our churches much like we run our businesses. We have a CEO who runs the management teams. Management then runs the employees. I understand governmental order and praying over spiritual matters, but when a person is the topic of conversation and you have not gone one on one with them then you have slaughtered their reputation and harmed their character. God's church is not a business, it is a spiritual body uniquely put together by the Father as a bride for the Son. We have been given protocols on how to conduct ourselves as a family of God, not as a business. You will never fully stop gossip because we all still wrestle with our flesh and I too get caught up sometimes and have to repent. However, we need to make a conscience effort to do church God's way and not the worlds way.

Sadly, my journey to find Jesus came with more heartbreak. We eventually left this ministry the lack of love was no longer tolerable. The ministry treated people very poorly. After leaving I found out three days later the Senior Pastor was having an affair with his good friends' wife. This solidified to me why the love was not there. It was another sold out compromised religious church in the name of Jesus. The congregation kept him in his position proving the state of our churches are very broken inside the buildings we call church in America.

I realized Jesus is not lost many of the professing Christians are lost. Jesus warned the road was narrow and few be them that find it. He wasn't kidding many will stand before Him saying Lord and He will say, "Depart from me, I never knew you."

WOULD THE REAL JESUS PLEASE STAND UP?

*H*ave you ever seen that game show *To Tell the Truth,* the one where three people all represent one person? Only one of the people were actually the real person. The contestants would ask various questions and by the end they had to guess which one was the real person being represented. Most of my Christian life or experience has been feeling like I am playing that game.

The Jesus I had wanted in my life was the one who would make me rich. I started my own business when I was just twenty years old. I wanted good health, lots of wealth and my best life now. I loved luxury. I was full of pride and ego. I loved how people treated me as a young woman in business. I had nice cars and big fancy house in the affluent part of town. I was one of the first people to have a cell phone. I always dressed in name brand clothes. My hair and nails were always perfect. I was what you called "high maintenance." I believed these were the blessings of Jesus.

I paid my tithes and offerings expecting that God would give me more and more. He was my 401'J', Jesus was my investment, my insurance policy to remain rich and prosperous. I even taught Christian finance classes to help others get debt free and wealthy.

My teachers were all health wealth and prosperity teachers. I did not want to know about sin. I wanted to float around on my Jesus cloud all day. I would speak things into existence like I was told too. The sad thing is it worked for material things. Internally I was miserable. I was bound up and living in my own personal hell. However, on the outside I had what seemed to be the perfect life. Fancy vacations, great kids, awesome husband, big house everyone admired, drove nice cars. I thought all of this was truly because Jesus loved me, and I was blessed by Him.

While I was on my journey to find Jesus, I realized much of these things can actually be part of the strong delusion. My "perfect" life kept me in the delusion that I was "saved."

God will sometimes allow your desires to be met to make you continue in your delusion, since you refused to believe the truth.

In the same way false teachers are our judgment to the "church" for refusing to read the bible for ourselves and follow the right Jesus. I know what I am saying is not popular. I know we all want to believe all good things come from God. God is good! God is great, actually. However, just because someone is blessed with material blessings does not mean they have Gods favor or His salvation.

Do not misunderstand me. God gives good gifts to His kids. I am still blessed today. Now my heart has changed though. I don't seek after the big fancy house now; I don't drive the fancy cars now. I have not been on a vacation in probably ten years or better. When I travel now it's for missions. Everything I am blessed with I ask myself how this can be used to make Christ known.

When I studied the life of the Jesus, the apostles, the early church I did not see prosperity. I saw persecution. I saw outcasts. I saw men and women risking everything to make Christ known to the world. Somewhere along the way we have forgotten our purpose here as the church of God.

EVALUATING THE JESUS OF SCRIPTURE

Jesus said about following Him:

> *"Then Jesus told his disciples, "if anyone would come after Me, let him deny himself and take up his cross and follow Me."*

> — *MATTHEW 16:24*

> *"and whoever does not take his cross and follow Me is not worthy of Me"*

> — *MATTHEW 10:38*

Jesus expects His followers to deny their fleshly desires. To put their flesh to death and pick up the cross. The cross represented death, curse, persecution, being an outcast, not following the in-crowd. Pick up our cross means not being like everyone else.

> *"and you will be hated by all for My name's sake. But the one who endures to the end will be saved."*

> — *MATTHEW 10:22*

Jesus is saying we will be hated for His Names sake. That means everything He represents is what we should represent. Since we represent Him, we need to expect to be hated. This does not mean we are out looking for fights but once you preach the truth of the gospel we will be under attack. When we stand for what the scripture teaches and refuse to compromise, we will be persecuted.

"Jesus said to him, "If you would be perfect, go sell what you possess and give to the poor, and you will have treasure in heaven; and come, follow Me.""

— MATTHEW 19:21

"Now great crowds accompanied him, and he turned and said to them, "If anyone comes to me and does not hate his own father and mother and wife and children and brothers and sisters, yes, and even his own life, he cannot be my disciple. Whoever does not bear his own cross and come after me cannot be my disciple. For which of you, desiring to build a tower, does not first sit down and count the cost, whether he has enough to complete it? Otherwise, when he has laid a foundation and is not able to finish, all who see it begin to mock him, saying, 'This man

began to build and was not able to finish.' Or what king, going out to encounter another king in war, will not sit down first and deliberate whether he is able with ten thousand to meet him who comes against him with twenty-thousand? And if not, while the other is yet a great way off, he sends a delegation and asks for terms of peace. So therefore, any one of you who does not renounce all that he has cannot be my disciple."

— LUKE 14:25-33

What is Jesus saying here? He is letting us know that following Him could cost us our family and friends. When we become born again everything changes. We no longer laugh at the jokes we used to laugh at. We do not desire drinking, parties, rated R movies or the sexual immorality.

We become the light that exposes the darkness now. (Ephesians 5:11)

Our family will likely feel uncomfortable around us or treat us differently. Our unsaved friends will have nothing in common with us anymore. (2 Corinthians 6:14)

We love our family, and we desire for them to be saved, however, we have a brand-new family. We have new brothers and sisters in the kingdom of God. (Mark 3:31-35)

Jesus is telling us to count the cost of following Him.

We need to really think about what it might cost us. Not only could it cost us our family and friends, but it may cost us our job, may cost us to give up the world's pleasures. Maybe we are really wealthy, and God says downsize and give more to the gospel. Maybe He said sell the fancy cars and drive a winter beater.

He had me do that for a period of time. I purchased a little green 1997 Honda with a smashed-in side door. I drove this car for three years. It humbled me. I had people look at me with disdain. People would pull up beside me in their luxurious rides and just look at me and put their nose in the air. I would laugh because I had money to go buy a new car, but He was developing something in me, humility.

He was teaching me about being rooted in Him for acceptance. I had a lot of pride and He wanted it smashed out of me. I drove that little green monster (this is what I called it) until it died. I ended up giving it to a family in need. They were able to fix it for cheap and they drove it for a while. I still do not have a car of my own to drive. I drive whatever vehicle is available in my driveway but none of them are "my style" or "my vehicle." I have a van I drive around to pick people up and take to church. My husband has a work truck and a work car. I drive whichever is available. I no longer put my identity in what I drive.

Let's examine a man named Nicodemus that Jesus encountered. He was the greatest teacher in Israel at that time. The story is in John Chapter 3.

Now there was a man of the Pharisees named Nicodemus, a ruler of the Jews.

This man came to Jesus by night and said to him, "Rabbi, we know that you are a teacher come from God, for no one can do these signs that you do unless God is with him."

Jesus answered him, "Truly, truly, I say to you, unless one is born again] he cannot see the kingdom of God."

Nicodemus said to him, "How can a man be born when he is old? Can he enter a second time into his mother's womb and be born?"

Jesus answered, "Truly, truly, I say to you, unless one is born of water and the Spirit, he cannot enter the kingdom of God. That which is born of the flesh is flesh, and that which is born of the Spirit is spirit. Do not marvel that I said to you, 'You must be born again. The wind blows where it wishes, and you hear its sound, but you do not know where it comes from or where it goes. So, it is with everyone who is born of the Spirit."

Nicodemus said to him, "How can these things be?"

Jesus answered him, "Are you the teacher of Israel and yet you do not understand these things? Truly, truly, I say to you, we speak of what we know, and bear witness to what we have seen, but you do not receive our testimony. If I have told you earthly things and you do not believe, how can you believe if I tell you heavenly things no one has ascended into heaven except he who descended from heaven, the Son of Man. And as Moses lifted up the serpent in the wilderness, so must the Son of Man be lifted up, that whoever believes in him may have eternal life.

Nicodemus recognizes Jesus is different and that He must come from God because He has never seen anything like this is the way of miracles and His teachings. Nicodemus would have worked so hard to become the prestigious pharisee that he was. He worked extremely hard to keep the law; he memorized all the scriptures he needed too. He taught in the synagogue.

He was revered among the Jewish people as a great leader. He had arrived in his religion.

Being born again is a supernatural work from God; where the Holy Spirit regenerates you.

Here is Jesus telling him that all of his works do not matter. He has to be born again. Not only born again but it can only come from God above. He can't earn it. He can't work for it. Basically, all that work you have done to get where you are does not matter Nicodemus, you must be born again. We must repent and place our faith in Christ, the Messiah.

Finding out his works were meaningless likely devastated Nicodemus. However, tradition has said that he did go on to become born again. He lost everything. Tradition says that when he became a follower of Christ he was excommunicated from the Jewish temple as well as Jewish society. He lost all his wealth and his good name. Losing everything not only affected him but his entire family for generations.

Jesus made it very clear that following Him will cost us. He may call you to the mission field, to a dangerous mission field. He may call you to singleness. He may ask you to remain in a hard marriage. He may call you into a hard neighborhood. I don't know but He says count the cost before following Him. We are not used to that here in America but around the world they do know that following Christ can mean loss of family, tradition, wealth, stature and even your life. For example, if a Muslim man or woman converts to Christianity, they understand it will cost them everything in their culture and depending on where they live likely their life.

The real Jesus is one of radical obedience to the mission. He only did the will of the Father. He came to reconcile people back to the Father. He was a reformer of the religious institution in His earthly ministry. He came to give truth. He demonstrated truth by example and by power. He never backed down; He taught the truth all the way to the cross. He then rose again and continued to teach truth until His ascension. He still teaches us today through His word empowered by His Holy Spirit.

Are we listening?

Do we really get what biblical Christianity is?

Have we chosen the wrong Jesus?

Are we just playing church?

Would the real Jesus please stand up!

PLAYING CHURCH

*A*s the years dragged on, I found myself hopeless and wondering what is this Christian thing anyway I read about in the bible. I started to realize most of us are playing church. I think it's an unconscious thing. I don't believe people wake up on Sundays get all dressed up and say to themselves "let's go play church today." I think rather many of us are under a strong delusion and are not self-evaluating why we do what we do, what kind of attitude do we bring to it and is it truly because we are passionately in love with Jesus and His chosen bride.

Do we want holiness?

Do we want a family that holds us accountable?

Do we want to be pushed higher towards Him?

Do we really want the Jesus of scripture?

Do we want to lay our lives down for the people who sit next to us on Sunday?

I made playing church look really good. I was the queen of playing church. No one who knew me would think I was not saved, I professed Christ, I never denied Him. I taught Christian classes, I gave money, I attended church often.

Later in my false conversion I attended regularly and was in leadership roles. I carried my bible and even read the Psalms and Proverbs. I attended "Christian conferences" and had myself fully convinced of my salvation.

I was just doing what I was told to do my whole life by my grandma. I was doing what millions of American Christians do every week. We go to church, we serve, we pay our tithe, we live seemly decent lives then we die and go to heaven. Most of our Christianity is displayed in a few hours on a Sunday maybe a Wednesday Night and the occasional party, picnic, or function the church hosts.

I didn't realize I was playing church at the time.

I used church to please my grandma.

I used church to make me feel better about my sin.

I used church to feel like a place I can serve and use my gifts.

However, church was never a community to me. It

never felt like a family. I never felt like these people would lay their lives down for me. Nor would I lay my life down for them. I couldn't find anyone who even wanted to come along side me and teach me the word of God. Someone who would sacrifice their time to do life with me. Jesus spent three and half years intricately connected to His disciples. Paul spent three years discipling the people in Ephesus. Timothy was with Paul most of his youth until being released into ministry. This is the pattern of biblical discipleship. I desired it deeply but could not find it.

I saw so many people inside these buildings living just like the world. I saw backbiting and gossip. I saw pride and egos. I saw many shady things. I myself was in extreme bondage so who was I to judge really.

I was just like them.

We often use the word "churchianity" when we speak about playing church.

Churchianity: *Any practice of Christianity that are viewed as placing a larger emphasis on the habits of church life or the institutional traditions of the church than on theology and spiritual teachings of Jesus; the quality of being too church-focused OR BUILDING FOCUSED*

I have seen it everywhere I have gone. People who profess Christ but by their fruit you wonder, why are they even here? Why do you come to church? Why are you serving? Why are you behind the pulpit? Why are you on the worship team? Why are you teaching children? Why do you take communion? Why do you even come at all when you live so opposite of the word every other day?

I know for me I came to church because I feared hell, I had someone to please, I was taught this is what you do in America, it made me feel better about my sin, I believed God would bless me more with money and things, and I thought He would protect me and my family from bad things happening. Jesus said If I deny Him before man, He will deny me before the Father, so I did my "works" to prove I would not deny Him.

"but whoever denies Me before men, I also will deny before My Father who is in Heaven"

— *MATTHEW 10:33*

I cannot judge the motives of anyone's heart. I just know that by their attitude fruit I wonder if they are truly in love with Jesus. I was deceived and under a strong delusion myself. I understand the false converts heart because I was that person for so long. My heart aches like you wouldn't believe when I see myself in so many others on Sundays or in our culture. The heart is deceitfully wicked and we can justify anything our flesh desires when we are not truly regenerated.

ARE YOU PLAYING CHURCH?

MY EXPERIENCES:

My first memory was of a "youth pastor" when I was in Jr. High. He was young and single and started fooling around with my 8th grade friends. I didn't attend church regularly and this was actually the church my friend attended. All my friends were getting into drinking and boys; and this "youth pastor" was considered cool, so they all went to his class on Wednesdays. There is nothing cool about calling yourself a pastor and condoning sin and fooling around with underage girls who look up to you.

What was it then?

Why was he a youth pastor?

Could it be he was raised in church or in the ministry, so he felt obligated to go into ministry for the "family business"? Could it be he loved the title and power being a pastor brings you? Could it be the money? I have no idea, but what I do know is he was playing church.

My first pastor as an adult baptized me and my boyfriend in water knowing we were living together and had a daughter out of wedlock. He never spoke to us about sexual immorality. He never told me the scriptures about sexually immoral people will not inherit the kingdom of God. He baptized me knowing I was going to go right back into the same sin I was supposedly turning from. I had no repentance. Baptism to me was just a religious event Christians are commanded to do. Had he judged my fruit he would clearly know I was not a born-again creation in Christ.

"Or do you not know that the unrighteous will not inherit the kingdom of God? DO NOT BE DECEIVED: neither the sexually immoral, nor idolaters, nor adulterers, nor men who practice homosexuality, nor thieves, nor the greedy, nor drunkards, nor revilers, nor swindlers will inherit the kingdom of God."

— 1 CORINTHIANS 6:9-10

He also had us dedicate our baby in front of the church. I now understand that dedicating a child in front of the church says I am going to raise that baby in the ways of the Lord. I promise to bring her up through the word of God, among the family of God. I myself will live a life of separation onto God for my child to pattern after.

He never explained this to me. I was again living with her dad out of wedlock. We left the church that day just as we had after our baptisms going right back into fornication, drinking, parties, worldly lusts, and desires. We did what we knew our grandparents and parents wanted. We knew that it was a good thing to be in church. However, the night before we were at bars partying and living, acting, looking, talking just like the rest of the world. I was breaking the very promise I just kept in front of the congregation because no one taught me otherwise.

Another time when I was 20 years old, I wanted to lead a Christian health class. I had to do it through a church per the rules of the health organization. I went to the church that I barely attended and asked the pastor if I could lead the class. He gave me permission without hesitation. I had many women from his church coming to my class. Looking back on this that was not wise of the pastor. I was living in the bars on Saturdays, barely going to church on Sundays and lived just like the world. It seems harmless but people look up to you whenever you are teaching anything or leading anything. His answer to me should have been no. He should have evaluated my walk with Christ not my profession. He should have insisted I was a faithful attender and inspected my fruit over a long period of time. He should have asked one of his mature women to lead the class and allow me to attend it. I can't even imagine what my life may have been like if someone took the time to labor through the scriptures with me in love with the intentions of my soul being saved.

Shortly after that, we were out of church and living life. I would get urges to go to church every once in a while. My grandma would always ask me if I went to church, and she would be so disappointed when I would say no. I would go just to make her proud. Also, I had convinced myself I loved Jesus and was a Christian, so I went to church sometimes to prove it.

We eventually got married and then divorced. We were so young, and both came out of such brokenness. I had developed PTSD and panic attacks during our marriage. Not because of him, but rather my traumatic childhood.

I met my current husband and of course professed Christ but was again fornicating and going to church. He wasn't saved though; he too professed Christ, just like I did.

We went to a church down the street, and we liked it, so we thought we would become members. We took the membership classes and got semi involved in the church. It was time to sign for membership and the pastor took us in his office to talk. He said that because were living together and not married that there were some "old people" in the church that would frown upon us being members. He wanted to make it clear they had religious spirits and that he whole heartily disagreed with them. Matter of fact he made it known that he had no problem at all our living arrangements he just didn't want to upset the "old timers."

What did all these "Senior Pastors" do? They condoned our sin. They winked at our sin. They didn't love us enough to warn us that the road is narrow, and few be them that find it. They didn't warn us that Jesus said on Judgement Day many would come to Him saying His name twice and yet He would say He never knew them; they were lawless workers of sin. (Matthew 7:21-23) If we would have left those churches and got in a deadly car accident we would be in hell for all eternity.

I cry as I write this story. My heart still breaks. What if someone had enough love to sit me down and warn me that my fruit did not line up with my profession. That *just maybe* I wasn't really born again. I needed to repent of my sin, turn away from it and receive the free gift of eternal salvation which then is evidenced by a transformed life.

These pastors were playing church. I don't know if they are saved, all I know is they played with my soul. They didn't take their mandate as overseers seriously. They saw church as a business, as a job, as something other than what church is. Souls are at stake and we have to start telling people the truth in love. We can't continue like this saint of God.

My story is over 20 years ago, how much worse has it gotten since then?

I wish these were the only two stories I had about pastors. However, I have many many more. Everywhere I go I see pastors and elders winking at sexual sin. One pastor was single and sleeping with the women in the church. He ended up getting one pregnant so married her quickly hoping no one would notice the baby was born full term 3 months earlier than the "due date".

Another pastor had a worship leader preying on the women in the congregation. He would use them for sex, give them scripture on why it was ok to fornicate. He forced them to watch porn and degraded them. He especially loved the young ones. He was an anointed singer/songwriter to an exceptionally large ministry so keeping up appearances on stage was particularly important to the Pastor. I only found out because one of the women came to me for counseling. When the pastor was confronted, he said he knew all about the worship leader, he excused his sin as a weakness he can't seem to overcome. The leader remained in his position, he is still today abusing women sexually and leading worship. According to him many on that stage do the same thing.

Another pastor was addicted to porn and emailing mail order brides. He treated his wife like a sex object and abused her emotionally. I wish this wasn't the norm, but it seems to be now. Many Pastors that claim to be pastors for twenty years yet have cheated on their wives, alcohol binges, porn addiction, abuse the sheep, lie, gossip and slander; I have seen it all.

This isn't easy for me to write. I am embarrassed and angered by the state of the church. Many sheep are being slaughtered in the name of Christ because of these men and women playing church. We wink at this heinous sin and say "oh they are saved it's just the flesh is weak" or "they lost their salvation during that time, but they got it back" I am not here to argue theology right now but that is just not biblical.

*"No one born of God makes a practice of sinning,
for God's seed abides in him; and he cannot keep on
sinning, because he has been born of God."*

— *1 JOHN 3:9*

These men are in willful habitual unrepentant sin
for periods of time. We can all fall short and mess up. I
am talking about blatant long-term sin. Sin that's not
been revealed or repented of. Especially in an elder.
Elders are held to a higher standard and church
discipline must be enacted at the strictest level.

*"As for those who persist in sin, rebuke them in the
presence of all, so that the rest may stand in fear."*

— *1 TIMOTHY 5:20*

Once I finally attended church on a regular basis, I
worked my way from teaching the children all the way
up to head of women's ministry during my false
conversion era. How is that possible? It's possible
because many profess Christ and find themselves doing
things in His name for the wrong reasons. I did not ever
think during that time I wasn't saved. However, I never
learned the word of God for myself. I never lined my

life up with scripture. I never had a born-again experience that changed me from the inside out. I just did all the religious works that seemed right to do if you are a Christian. I never sought out truth. I never asked the hard questions. I was just in an assembly line of Christianity moving through the motions, telling myself I was ok.

Playing church for me was coming to church even doing good church deeds but never fully committing to the gospel. Would I die for Jesus? I mean not a gun to my head die, but die to myself? Would I sell everything and leave my family and friends to go preach the gospel in a tribe in Africa? Would I sell my fancy car, so I have more to give towards the poor? Did I really love people? I would give money because that was always easy for me to give but did I sacrifice my time? When I didn't get my own way was I rude? Did I gossip and judge people? Did I still love the bars, men, drinking, sexual sin like porn or fornication, overeating, secular music, rated R movies, expensive clothes, fancy vacations, materialism? Did I look more like the world than biblical Christianity? YES! The answer for me is YES! I was the definition of cultural Christianity.

WHAT IS CULTURAL CHRISTIANITY?

"Cultural Christianity is religion that superficially identifies itself as "Christianity" but does not truly adhere to the faith. A "cultural Christian" he wears the label "Christian," but the label has more to do with his family background and upbringing than any personal conviction that Jesus is Lord. Cultural Christianity is more social than spiritual."

— *GOT QUESTIONS MINISTRIES*

I grew in humanism or morally I matured; so I didn't go to bars anymore when I got married. However, now my focus was being the best suburban mom. My focus went from bar hopping to having the big house and fancy lifestyle. I no longer had sex outside of marriage because I had a certificate of marriage, but my heart was still full of lust towards my husband and sexual gratification. My heart had not changed in the way I looked at sex.

I share my testimony of my struggle with sexual sin on our YouTube channel.

https://bit.ly/MyStruggle_Amy

We can mature as we age. Our sin preference can change as we mature, however that doesn't make us born again with a new nature.

They had this supernatural encounter with God that changed them forever.

When I became regenerated by the Holy Spirit, born again or saved by God; I became a new person. We often talk about the transformed life of the drug addict or alcoholic. One day they came to church or a prayer meeting and cried out to God and from that day forward they never smoked or drank ever again. They suddenly had this new love for the people of God. They now want to give up everything to serve God. They laid down all they knew to pursue a radical love relationship with their Savior.

That's my story, my conversion is just as supernatural as the addict. I was the most heinous type of sinner. I had knowledge of God. I took His communion. I taught His people. I yoked up with His bride and saw my righteousness in my works not in His work. There was a stricter punishment awaiting me at Judgement Day, because I had access to the truth and refused to believe it or read it or live it. Instead I made excuses for my sin and rebellion. I justified my life as a church goer. I was the queen of playing church, I worked hard to earn that crown.

I have picked on pastors, but church members are just as guilty when winking at sin. We are supposed to go one on one. Iron sharpens iron. We are called to hold each other accountable and perfect each other towards Christ. I don't mean to make it all the elder's responsibility. Saints, its all of our responsibility to expect holiness among Gods body. We are all to walk in love and truth. Never do we go around criticizing each other, but if we see a family member stumbling or in great danger of falling off a cliff, do we not yell STOP?

These are people's eternal souls.

Hell is forever!

We must stop winking at sin and be bold enough with all the love and humility inside you to confront our brothers and sisters. I know it's hard, my stomach aches every time I have to go one on one. I shake and get all nervous. I also pray a lot about it and ask God to remove my own sin. I remind myself of my own imperfections and thank God for His grace and mercy.

We can think, is it really that bad? Have we become a church full of people not truly following Jesus?

I think of Judas. He was a man who was one of the 12 disciples. He was with Jesus for three and a half years. He saw all His miracles; he ate with Him. Judas would have experienced dynamic teachings. The love and compassion Judas would have felt from Jesus would be transforming. Jesus cast out demons. He raised Lazarus from the dead! Jesus healed lepers and lame people. Apostle John writes that there were so many miracles the books of the world can't contain them, and Judas was a witness to it *all*.

Judas a man who walked with Jesus and yet he was playing church. He pretended to care for the poor when Mary anointed Jesus's body with oil that was worth a year's wages. Judas oversaw the treasury box. Some believe Judas ate the wine and bread. Judas even kissed Jesus and called Him Master as he revealed to the soldiers who Jesus was.

I prayed about this and pictured walking with Jesus Himself. I pictured being taught directly from Jesus, seeing all His miracles, experiencing the love He would have demonstrated. I can't imagine playing church for as long as I did, had I been with Jesus like that. It made me question that if Judas who physically was with Jesus could play church, how much more can those who have never seen or experienced Jesus in this way play church?

If the Jesus ratio for people playing church is 1/12, how much more could our ratio be, especially in America where it seems to cost us so little. Billy Graham one of the greatest crusaders of our modern history preached all over the world. In an interview in 1990 he admitted only about 25% who came forward actually became Christian. However, when evaluating their lives, it appears only 6% were actually any different in their lifestyle after one year (Myers, 2011).

Billy Graham preached the whole council of God. He preached repentance of sin and living a holy life. Today, we don't hear very many messages on repentance, sin, holiness, hell, or the whole council of God being represented.

Could our numbers be even lower in 2020?

We are rapidly declining as a Christian Nation in America. Poll in 2019 says only 65% identify as Christian. In 1990 it was 85% ("In U.S., decline of Christianity continues at rapid pace," 2020).

"It is my opinion that tens of thousands, if not million, have been brought into some kind of

religious experience by accepting Christ and they have not been saved."

— *A.W. TOZER*

In an article by Charisma News it is pointed out that other parts of the world Christianity are growing with new converts, in America conversions have declined. Only 2% of all churches are growing as a result of new conversions (Farias, 2017). The rest of the churches are either declining or flat lining.

When I read this statistic, I had to stop writing because I couldn't stop crying. How is it once the light on the hill, America is now converting the least number of Christians? Where did we go wrong? How did we become apathetic to the gospel? Who stole our zeal? Are we chasing another master such as money, success, fame, comforts? Are we institutionalized?

I grieve the state of the church today. I cry at times; I get mad at times and I want to quit at times. The rejection is intense, the hardened hearts and complacency burdens me to such a degree that it can overwhelm me. I do not in any way think I am better than my fellow church goer. On the contrary I was the complacent lukewarm false convert church goer for many years. I understand the delusion. I understand believing its ok to be like the world and profess Christ. My heart aches deep inside me when I see people professing Christ and baring the fruit of satan. **BeTheChurch** Ministry was started in hopes of helping people to stop playing church and actually become the church as described in the bible.

TIME FOR REFORMATION

I have a fire in me to see change in the church of God. To see His bride, return to her one true love, Jesus Christ. We are referred to as the bride of Christ in the bible. Jesus is our Bridegroom who will come for us some day and take us home with Him to live forever. I want to see her return to the love of His word and a desire to obey it.

The word reformer means someone who tries to change and improve something such as a law or social system. Synonyms would be reformist, crusader, and a social reformer.

When I read about reformers in Christian History, I admire their boldness to go up against the giants of their day in order to be biblically correct.

I admire the men and women willing to put

everything on the line to live biblically—to go up against powerful forces that are not living as the bible has commanded. I believe God has allowed me to experience all the dysfunction inside the church buildings to be a part of bringing reformation to His church. To be a leader in calling God's people back to the basic principles of Christianity, these stories I am about to tell you inspire me to continue to fight for truth. We can't give up seeking reformation in the church of God. We are soldiers in Gods army prepared to fight for His truth. We are prepared to fight for His word.

JOHN WYCLIFFE

John Wycliffe was one of the first reformers in our history. He was born in 1330 and went to be with the Lord in 1384. John Wycliffe was a man passionate about reading God's word. He produced some of the first handwritten English translations of our bible. He also made it his mission to get them into the hands of the common people.

Wycliffe criticized the papacy of the Catholic church for many of their unbiblical practices, such as the power of man in the church and their concern with secular power as well. This power caused them to act immorally as overseer of the church of God and it appalled him. He wrote against indulgences for forgiveness of sin.

He angered the Catholic church and they tried to have all the English bibles burned but because he had such a powerful street team, they could not burn them all. Many bibles went out into the marketplace among common people giving people the opportunity to read the word for themselves.

Twenty years after his death the Catholic church deemed him a heretic and had his body exhumed and his bones crushed.

JAN HUS

Jan Hus born 1369 and went to be with the Lord after being burned at the stake in 1415. Hus became greatly influenced by the writings of Wycliffe. He found many of the same issues in the Catholic church after reading and studying the bible for himself.

Jan Hus preached against adding works to salvation such as obeying church rules or good works, selling of indulgences to get loved ones out of purgatory sooner, also the power of the overseers to charge money for their work and the power and influence they had over people and land ownership. He also preached that the bible is our final authority not the pope.

Needless to say, preaching out against the truth especially if it effected their money and power caused him to be excommunicated and burned at the stake.

MARTIN LUTHER

Martin Luther born 1483 and went to be with the Lord 1546 is considered the father of the Protestant reformation. Luther was a German monk and actually loved the catholic church very much. However, in reading the bible for himself he too discovered the church was apostate from biblical Christianity.

Luther preached against the pope being infallible. He also agreed with Wycliffe and Hus that the bible is our final authority in all matters not man, not the pope, not the church doctrines. He really tried to get the church to see its errors and had no desire to divide with them. After several attempts he nailed the 95 theses on the door of the Castle Church in Wittenberg on October 31st, 1517. He challenged everything from indulgences, faith alone in Christ, and the pope being so wealthy.

Luther went on to write pamphlets expressing the truth of scripture and why the Catholic church was not biblical. He spread these pamphlets all around

Germany. Because the printing press was newly invented Luther was able to mass produce his writings and get them circulated much faster. He was eventually excommunicated and lived a life as an outlaw from the Catholic church. However, his truth teachings spurred on what we now know is the protestant reformation.

KATHARINA LUTHER

Katharina Luther born 1499 and went to be with the Lord 1552 was a woman of great influence during the beginning years of the reformation. We don't often read much about the women behind these great men. Martin would write his works and she was known to read them in the evenings and give her input. She turned her home into a place of education for children and Martin's students to further the gospel. She kept a home ready for travelers with food and fresh linen.

Many of the women were known for turning their homes into schools and travel lodges to further the protestant movement. They worked hard while they cooked, cleaned, taught, and even ran food pantries out of their homes. Many affluent women such as Queens and princesses converted to Protestantism. They became targets from the Catholic church and ended up living isolated lives under extreme intimidation. Many suffered violence and persecution.

Women also used the pen to influence the reformation. They would write educational pieces and works to help with literacy. Many would write pieces on theology and doctrine. Their works were published and distributed. Poetry was a common form of writing for the women of the reformation. They would pen their own journeys from Catholicism to what may be recognized as Calvinism or faith alone in Christ alone theology.

MODERN DAY REFORMERS

A.W. Tozer

A.W. Tozer born 1887 and went home to be with the Lord 1963. Tozer was a man who had the guts to say the hard things. He saw the move towards immorality in America. He was wise beyond his years. Tozer had no formal Christian education yet only after 5 years of being a Christian he pastored his first church. He went on to pastor for 44 years.

Tozer was passionate to get God's people to develop a more personal serious relationship with God. Holiness was often a topic he preached on. You can read many of his compilations in "The Pursuit of God" and "The Knowledge of the Holy One." Tozer understood the loneliness and isolation for preaching the hard truths of the bible. He would express in his sermons and writings the hard-narrow road of being a Christian.

Tozer lived a simple life. He never owned a car and signed away much of his royalties for his writings to the poor. He lived a life of prayer and through his prayers would extend his writings and his teachings.

DAVID WILKERSON

David Wilkerson born 1931 and went to be with the Lord in 2011. Wilkerson was a passionate preacher of God's word. Many of his teachings were exposing the apostate church. He called people inside the churches to repent. He desired that Christ's teachings be center of the Christian walk and that we should obey them. Wilkerson did not sugar coat God's holiness and God's love. Wilkerson did not care for denominations but rather wanted us to unite as a bride of Christ. The bride he often talked about was one of holiness and obedience to Christ. He was concerned that much of the church had become apostate.

Wilkerson was not afraid to go into the hi-ways and bi-ways and preach Jesus to even the most hardened criminals. He was known for his bold preaching to gang members and at-risk teens. He had a passion for the young generation and wanted them to know Jesus is the answer not drugs, alcohol, or sexual immorality. His passion was to make Christ known, not only in America but across the world. Even though his ministries grew into worldwide successes he never compromised the message of holiness in Christ and did not back down on calling out the apostate church especially in America.

Wilkerson seemed to be prophetic as he could see the changing morality in America and especially the compromise of the American church. It grieved him deeply and he never backed down calling her out of her Luke warmness and into a right relationship with Jesus that lines up with scripture.

PAUL WASHER

Paul Washer born 1961 currently still preaching the gospel. Washer is known for his passionate preaching in the American churches. Watch any of his YouTube sermons and you can't help but be convicted. Washer was a missionary in Peru when God called him back to the United States to preach the gospel to the church. He has been known to preach such a biblical truth message that brings such conviction on the heart of man that he is not welcomed back into some churches.

Washer is still deeply involved in missions abroad but also knows he has a burden for the apostate church in America. He is a popular preacher in his own circles, but the lukewarm church is very offended by him. He is known as the crying pastor because he grieves so much for the church of God and her great falling away.

His body is full of metal due to the harsh conditions he has lived under as a missionary and yet nothing stops him from continuing the gospel work. He understands the rejection from man when you preach the truth to a church that seems to no longer except the truth. I doubt he would call himself a reformer but, in my book, he has gone against the tide in American Christianity and not been afraid to call her out of her complacency and her compromise. God used brother Paul Washer to open my eyes to my own false conversion many years ago. Although he may never know it until we reach heaven, and I am beyond grateful for his ministry.

SPIRIT OF REFORMATION

There is a long list of reformers throughout church history and even today. I recommend reading the "Foxes book of Martyrs" by John Foxe. It depicts many men and women who have sacrificed their lives for the gospel. They went up against apostate churches, governments, families and more to preach the true gospel of Jesus Christ. They paid the highest price, their life.

I want to start another reformation.

As I mentioned earlier, I have a reformation spirit that burns within me. I want to see the church turn back to biblical, sold out, radical love and holiness Christianity. If there was only one church per city, I would nail a thesis on each door. "This is what the Lord and His word have against you."

I love the bride of Christ. I lay my life down daily for His sheep in the way of discipleship. It crushes me to speak against the church. However, what we call church in America has quickly become the church which has greatly fallen away.

I believe God is stirring a reformation in His bride as we are fast approaching the last days. I meet people from all over that seem to really connect with the understanding of BeTheChurch. They see the church is not working for people as a whole. They are hungry for more but not quite sure how to come out from among the tares and be the church.

I ask God how can this small group of people from northern Ohio make a difference? I felt Him press upon me, one soul at a time Jesus only had 12. The other important aspect of being the church is being the example. We have two hashtags we often say #BeTheChurch and #BeTheExample.

Can you relate to feeling like a reformer? Do you believe God may be calling you to be a part of the change needed in our modern Christianity?

Are you willing to be persecuted especially from other church members?

Do you desire change?

Does rejection seem to follow you?

Do you burn with sadness and anger towards the complacency of the church?

Do you often feel like you want to flip tables and call out the injustice?

Are you tired of fluffy Jesus sermonettes that are not equipping the saints or pointing to Christ alone? Are you tired of watered-down messages and out of context sermons? Does it grieve you that people come and go inside these buildings with no real change in their lives?

Do you often ask, "What is the point Lord, we look and act just like the world"?

Are you tired of having to wear a mask to church

because no one really wants to know how you are doing? If they do care it's often so they have something to talk about. Does all the sexual immorality inside the church walls grieve your spirit? Do you feel alone in your thinking? When you read the bible do you find yourself longing for the church described in Acts chapter two? Do you feel tired? Do you just want Jesus to return because the problem has gotten so big that it seems there is not hope? Do you feel like your spirit is often stirred for something so much more but then is quenched because you can't really find that tribe of people who feel it too?

God wants to use you to make a difference in the church.

If you are relating to any of this it's likely you are a reformer. He is calling His bride to stand up for righteousness. He is calling His bride back to biblical Christianity where He is the head. We believe God is stirring up a reformation even bigger than the protestant movement. Not because what they did was small, it's because the problem is that much larger.

We have more than one universal church to confront. We have churches on almost every street corner. We have entire denominations going apostate it seems monthly or yearly. We are in the fight of our lives saint but He who is in us is greater than He who is in the world. Pick up your sword, let's contend together for truth.

It is time for another reformation.

BETHECHURCH

What does that mean to *Be the Church*? For us it simply means living out the biblical church. We hold to the scriptures as what church was meant to be. We love Jesus, we love people, and we make Christ known.

And they devoted themselves to the apostles teaching and the fellowship, to the breaking of bread and the prayers. And awe came upon every soul, and many wonders and signs were being done through the apostles. And all who believed were together and had all things in common. And they were selling their possessions and belongings and distributing the proceeds to all, as any had need. And day by day, attending the temple together and breaking bread in their homes, they received their food with glad and generous hearts, praising God and having favor with all the people. And the Lord added to their number day by day those who were being saved.

— ACTS 2: 42-47

The body was devoted to the apostles' teachings which is the word of God for us. The early church clung to the letters, clung to the old testament writings learning about Jesus. They did not meet for a couple hours on Sunday but rather they spent time together all week long. They did life together. They were a family.

Becoming a follower of "The Way" as it was called or becoming a Christian often meant you lost your family, friends, rights to the temple even your job was in jeopardy. They were a family and they laid everything down for each other and for the gospel to be spread throughout. They were so unified in Christ. The love they had for each other was so obvious to the outside world. They became this tight knit community that just celebrated Christ together. They walked in power and love which God added to them daily new believers.

Have you longed for this? Have you often wondered why were they so different than what we experience here 2000 plus years later?

When I became truly born again, I would cry out to God for help with all the problems I had seen with the church today. I would cry, "Lord, once we preach the gospel where do we send them for discipleship?" We had traveled to so many different churches and denominations and it seemed few had the discipleship in place, the reverence for God's word, the standard of biblical morality and holding each other accountable to it or a sold-out sacrificial love for the body of Christ.

I remember being in my study crying because it felt like it's way too big for me to tackle. I can sometimes relate to Martin Luther when he realized after reading the bible for himself that his religion was wrong. Can you imagine facing that kind of giant? Loving your faith so much loving the people of God with your entire being and yet realizing we have become so far from biblical Christianity. From what I have studied of Luther it seemed he was faced with just that giant, a true love for the church but a battle to make them see they have become apostate. I do not believe all of the churches are apostate in America. I attend and am apart of many great ministries who love Jesus. However, as a whole modern American Christianity is in a crisis for truth.

The giant Luther and many others have faced as they had to stand for truth would have felt like a huge obstacle. Many today see the problem but are too afraid to speak out against it or they just have grown apathetic to it. I think of the giant Kind David faced. David was small in stature but mighty in spirit. He took down lions and bears as a good shepherd. Now he would face the greatest giant. One who threatened Israel, God's people. David was not afraid because he knew who His God was. The Lord of Hosts. Lord of Hosts means God as Lord over earthly and heavenly armies.

I feel like David, this small little force against this machine of churchianity. I realize that we are in the end days. Paul warned of a great falling away.

Now concerning the coming of our Lord Jesus Christ and our being gathered together to him, we ask you, brothers, not to be quickly shaken in mind or alarmed, either by a spirit or a spoken word, or a letter seeming to be from us, to the effect that the day of the Lord has come Let no one deceive you in any way. For that day will not come, unless the rebellion comes first, and the man of lawlessness is revealed, the son of destruction.

— 2 THESSALONIANS 2:1-3

Jesus asked if there would be any faithful when He returned.

I tell you; he will give justice to them speedily. Nevertheless, when the Son of Man comes, will he find faith on earth?"

— LUKE 18:8

I know we can't change the trajectory of the return of Christ however, I do believe we need to walk as He commanded us to walk until He returns. Just like all the reformers past we need to have the boldness to stand up against apostasy and things that are not pleasing to the Lord who designed His church. We are not God, and we need to be humble about it. Among all this dysfunction is a beautiful bride of Christ who was hand chosen for the Son by the Father.

Often times what I see is my brothers and sisters starving for more. They are often wounded and tired. They love Jesus so much and feel like there should be more but seems that this is all God has for us. The lukewarm complacent church sold out too much of the world. Often, we feel isolated and alone in our pursuit of the Biblical Church. The church we read about in the scriptures seems to elude most of us.

When we try and be the church it seems we become offensive to the ones who just want to play church. They don't want held to a higher standard of living in holiness. They don't like that you won't gossip with them or participate in the church politics. Don't dare question the complacency of the church especially in regard to sin.

There is a solution saint. He's a huge giant but our God is a great big God. We often use the saying when ministering to people with large problems; "How do you eat an elephant"? Answer: One bite at a time

That's it, we can't change all of churchianity. We can't stop everyone from playing church. We can't possibly pluck out all the tares among the wheat nor is it our job. We can't always discern the goats from the sheep. Wolves are very crafty in their sheep clothing so we may not always know for sure who they are.

We are called to unify but it takes great love to do so.

If you are in a bible teaching church that holds to

orthodox teachings then I think we need to try and unify. I was bitten almost every week by "churchianity," but I look for the assignments from God and concentrate on those people.

I understand some of you are so church hurt and soon as I say unite--you say, "No Way! I will never go inside a building again!"

I feel you; I really feel you!

However, we are to be peacemakers. If you believe you are a true reformer then you are called to reform but also to unify. Martin Luther loved the church. He loved his faith. He loved his brothers and sisters, and his heart was not to bring disunity. His heart was hoping by giving them truth they would repent and turn from their false teachings and become the true biblical church again.

That did not work out so good for him. They excommunicated him and even wanted him dead. However, he started a movement called the "protest" or protestant movement. It's sad because now we "protest" every time something doesn't go our way and we start a new church or denomination.

BeTheChurch started out as an equipping ministry meant to compliment the church. We desire to be a support system and complement to our local churches.

What we saw through the years is many false converts like me playing church. We saw little to no discipleship. We saw little to no real inner healing or deliverance. We see little evangelism where the gospel is preached and lived out among the community.

Our vision is to preach the true gospel of Jesus Christ hoping that brings out salvation. We then walk them through inner healing as we all have lots of scars from our past. Last but not least we disciple them through the word of God. We equip them with the foundations of our Christian faith. We wrote a study guide to equip them with basic orthodox Christian theology. The study guide will help you find the answers to the questions below using the bible as our resource.

Who is God?

Who is Jesus?

What is salvation?

Why can we trust the bible?

Is hell real?

What about false religions such as Mormonism or Jehovah Witness?

What are the essential doctrines of our faith for salvation?

We have a local house church for those who desire a

more organic body ran environment with Elders in place to oversee. We have weekly and monthly outreaches to the lost where they learn to evangelize their faith. We host in home dinners and bible studies. We come together often and read the bible together, birthday parties, game nights, outreaches, weddings and more. We are a family; we are God's family.

We are a busy society which has made going house to house daily basis hard for some of us. We don't live close, we have kids, jobs, homes, etc. We stay connected daily through social media groups where we all talk and interact with each other throughout the day. Social media messenger groups have been a way for us to do life together on a daily basis. It has helped we have become a close-knit family. We simply love each other very much. We do our best to extinguish gossip and division for Love covers a multitude of sins even when we mess up, we are quick to forgive.

We have Arminian and Calvinists in the group. We have pre, mid and post tribbers (different ideas on when Jesus will return); flat earthers and round earthers, people who believe the revelatory gifts are for today and those who do not believe they are for today. We have vegans and meat eaters. We love that we are a diverse group of believers who are united in the essentials of the faith yet show each other Christian liberties in the non-essentials.

WHAT ARE THE CHRISTIAN BELIEFS FOR SALVATION IN ORTHODOX CHRISTIANITY?

The Deity of Christ: which is Jesus is God. We believe Jesus is fully God and also fully Man. John 10:30, John 20:28

Saved by faith alone in Christ alone by God's grace alone not by works of any kind. Ephesians 2:8-9 Christ is the only way to salvation Acts 4:12, John 14:6

Must believe in the Death, Burial and Resurrection of Jesus Christ 1 Corinthians 15:14, John 2:19-21

There is only one God, known as Monotheism Exodus 20:3

The Holy Trinity: One God operating in three distinct persons but yet One God. God the Father, God the Son and God the Holy Spirit Matthew 28:19, 1 Corinthians 12:4-6

The gospel as it has been presented in Scripture. There is only one saving gospel spelled out in scripture and so we must agree on what that gospel is. 1 Corinthians 15:1-4

Jesus born of a virgin Matthew 1:23

The bible is the pure word of God without

contradiction and is God breathed. The bible is our final authority as we hold everything to its authority.

You can learn more about the essential doctrines of salvation in our study guide "Equipping the Saints" found on Amazon or anywhere Christian books are sold.

BeTheChurch really is about uniting in Christ as discussed in Acts chapter 2 and 4. We have not sold everything we own as they did in the book of Acts, but we do give when others in the body have a need. We come together for the single mom, the sick child, the hurting wife or husband, the groceries, car repairs and physical sickness. We love Jesus and we love His word just like the early church.

We believe in holy living, being separated from the world.

We hold each other to the biblical moral standard of God's word. We love each other enough to help each other mature in Christ. We give each other a safe place to unmask when we are struggling with this flesh. We go one on one when we have an issue and keep that a biblical rule, we all follow by.

This keeps drama and chaos at bay. Overseers are not bogged down by gossip, drama, and carnality because we are teaching the biblical principles of how to interact as brothers and sisters in love and unity. God designed the body to be equally using their gifts for service as Christ our head directs us. Our Elders oversee and help guide us using scripture and pointing us always to Christ, the foundation of our faith.

COVID-19 SHUTDOWN

While finishing up this book COVID-19 hit. This brought a new level of fear onto the world. We prayed and asked God what would You have us to do during this time? I felt Him press upon our hearts "BE THE CHURCH." The needs didn't go away because the world stopped moving. Actually, the needs tripled as people found themselves out of work and relying on a broken unemployment system. The lines at the food pantries tripled in numbers, truckers couldn't get hot meals, elderly couldn't risk leaving their homes, single moms didn't want to take their young children to food lines and risk getting them sick.

Someone had to be on the front lines. Someone had to **BeTheChurch**. We saw most ministries close their doors and give no real assistance during this time. My heart ached as I started seeing brothers and sisters fighting online with one another. People calling each other names or judging each other for their convictions to stay open or closed. The saddest part was they used the bible to beat each other up.

Jesus called us to unite in love.

I had to hide many of my Facebook friends during this time as it took my peace. The devil divided God's people in a way I had never experienced. All I know is people were hurting and God called some to stay on the front lines to minister to the needs of the people even if it cost them their lives. Those who decided to stay home prayed for us daily. They were so instrumental in the ministry as they prayed us through the crisis.

I know there are conflicting emotions and information on whether churches should stay open or close. We stayed open for anyone who wanted to come take communion, worship God, or hear His word. We ministered to many people during this time and saw several come to saving faith. We never forced anyone to show up to our home, but we let everyone know our home was open to anyone in need. We took all the safety protocols, but we never stopped being the church.

God blessed our ministry in ways I cannot express. We tripled in donations, God added to the ministry souls for salvation, we became closer and more united then even before.

There were nights when we were in prayer and Gods tangible presence rested upon everyone in the room. It was so weighty we couldn't even move. We just sat/laid there and worshipped Him in silence. We prayed Psalm 91 as we gathered in small groups to worship Jesus.

I believe this season became a season of who's who. Those who I thought would be cheering on the people on the front lines became the biggest antagonist. I watched God use the "least of these" to be the reformers in our communities. He used the people society likes to disqualify to become the qualified. They went out and risked their lives to bring love and light to what seemed to be a hopeless time. I believe God is doing a new thing.

There will be an end time harvest like never seen before. God is bringing revival to His people, but it may look quite different than revivals in the past. He is coming back for a bride without spot and blemish and God is cleaning her up and preparing her for His return.

We are reformers!
We are His chosen Bride!
We are missionaries!
We were born for such a time as this!

During this time God had us purchase an outreach center. The food we were handing out was spread between five homes. We had supplies like coats, hats, gloves, socks, hygiene products etc. We needed a central location to house everything, and a place people could come anytime and receive what they need. We have a weekly food pantry now for anyone to get groceries from. We also have a 24/7 hotline for anyone in need.

We started a house church during COVID-19. We had every intention of going back to "normal" after it was over, and the church buildings would re-open. However, what was happening each week was so organic and beautiful we kept having weekly gatherings. We never advertised it and yet new people kept showing up. We do things a little differently than the modern church. We all sit in a circle and read through a letter of the bible together then open the discussion up for anyone to share their thoughts on the scripture read. The elders are present as they oversee the body operating in their gifts to make sure nothing is being taught that is contrary to scripture or that any disorder is arising.

We have become a family.

Each person has the ability and safe environment to use the gifts God has given them. The younger are being built up by the older in faith. After we worship and pray with each other and then have a nice communion meal together as a family. Many leave after dinner and many stay all day. We play games, fellowship, and just enjoy each other. As we continue to grow, we plan to raise up elders to start their own house churches.

We are not perfect, but we are seeing people grow in mighty ways. We are watching God use the foolish to profound the wise. We are seeing people so broken by sin become whole in Christ. Children being raised together like a real family. Mom's helping other moms, dad's helping other dads. We pattern our ministry after the early church as much as possible. We love God, Love People and are Making Christ Know!

What God is having us do can be done by others. We have laid our lives down for God's people and for humanity. It has cost us everything just as Jesus said it would. However, you too can **BeTheChurch**. You can do what we have done. It's a simple plan, though not easy. God is seeking willing hearts and if we just become willing, He will give the increase.

Are you willing?

*Do you desire to **BeTheChurch**?*

Are you longing for a family?

Contact us we would love to connect and see how we can encourage you.

MY PERSONAL LETTER TO THE CHURCH

To Whom it may concern,
I am deeply saddened. I am angry at the same time. I
wish I could say that since my own experiences of
church in the past several decades things have gotten
better, but alas I cannot. Things are continuing to get
worse. I am so tired of seeing men and women give
themselves titles or put themselves in positions or take
positions of authority but are not ready or able to really
tend to the souls of people. They want the title without
the dying to self.
Overseers are not to be dictators they are not in
"control," but they are to guide the souls towards
Christ. Their purpose to tend to the sheep until the
Good Shepherd returns for them. This is such a serious
job. Holy Spirit does guide us, and He does teach us,

and He does convict us, but God designed His church to also be a family. Overseers are like parents who help guide the younger ones to maturity towards Christ.

> *And he gave the apostles, the prophets, the evangelists, the shepherds and teachers, to equip the saints for the work of ministry, for building up the body of Christ, until we all attain to the unity of the faith and of the knowledge of the Son of God, to mature manhood, to the measure of the stature of the fullness of Christ, so that we may no longer be children, tossed to and fro by the waves and carried about by every wind of doctrine, by human cunning, by craftiness in deceitful schemes. Rather, speaking the truth in love, we are to grow up in every way into him who is the head, into Christ, from whom the whole body, joined and held together by every joint with which it is equipped, when each part is working properly, makes the body grow so that it builds itself up in love.*
>
> *— EPHESIANS 4:11-16*

We cannot wink at sin anymore overseers. If we do not have the guts to sit people down and express to them the seriousness of sexual sin inside the church, drinking parties, anger outbursts, pornography, lying, greed, gluttony then we are not fit for leadership. I do not care if we have been ordained, have PHD, or been behind a pulpit for one hundred years, if we are not taking the time to disciple the people God has entrusted us with and are not holding them accountable to biblical standards then we may be in trouble when we meet Jesus with blood of the souls all over our hands. I see young and old alike with no accountability to sexual sin inside the church. We walk them through all the rituals of our faith like baptism, communion, sinners' prayers, tithing and programs with little to no change happening. We think if we get them to jump enough of our religious hoops then that will help them grow.

Can they mature a little in humanism such as discipline or faithfulness to a system of rules? Sure, they can! Humans are capable of growing and maturing without being born again. However, what I have witnessed through the years is people who end up learning how to speak good Christian language, learn how to come to church, learn how to serve, learn how to smile, and hug, learn how to even serve at functions but they never learn about who God is. They have no real transformed life. They continue to have sex outside of marriage, they continue to party with the same friends they had before going to church, they still live look and act just like the world but now they put "God" as a cherry on top of their Facebook posts.

We have to stop playing with people's souls!

My greatest fear is that people God has put in our care as a spiritual mother will be standing in the line of Judgement Matthew 7:21-23 and say but Lord I went to **BeTheChurch** *studies every Friday, I helped them feed the homeless; I gave money to the ministry. My heart will break in two thinking what more could I have done. I understand the wheat grows up with the tares and there are goats among the sheep. However, I know each and every one of our members at* **BeTheChurch** *intimately. Could they be lying to me? Yes of course however rotten fruit eventually can't be hidden for a long period of time, it eventually starts to stink. God does tell us to know who we labor among. It is vital in a ministry to be good fruit inspectors.*

Overseers please start taking the time to pull back the wool of each of your people whom God has placed in your care. Ask the hard questions and give the biblical warnings. Implement church discipline if needed. If your church has grown to a point where you can no longer tend to the sheep properly then consider training others to be very intimate with the sheep as well.

We might consider starting smaller ministries instead of

these great big buildings to maintain. Maybe consider house churches with overseers in place of each house. I had a young girl die recently who was told she was saved because she repeated a prayer, got baptized and took communion. Yet by her own confession never felt any different. She continued down the road of destruction and sadly died a tragic death. Yet, the church who baptized her declared her saved because of "works" she performed by their prompting. We are not saved by religious works. God saves a man/woman and the evidence that He saved them is a transformed life. How dare us be so irresponsible with eternal souls. God forgive us for we have turned your grace into a common thing giving no expectation of holiness and damning people to a devil's hell in the Name of Jesus! We have to do better as God's overseers to tend to His sheep. No more excuses their eternal souls depend on it. I sadly cannot stop there.

*Church we have got to unify! We can't keep going on like this. Clicks, fractions, divisions are all among us. I see so much gossip. It's as if the church has no idea that the bible says, "Go one on one!" I have never seen this played out in all my years except in our ministry where it is a biblical mandate that we teach and adhere to. Our **BeTheChurch** family knows you are not to call me or anyone until you first went one on one with that* *person. Do you know how much fighting and division would stop right then if every single one of us made this a rule to live by?*

This starts with overseers. So often we think its ok to go to the pastor or leader first with our problem. No, the bible does not say that. We are all brothers and sisters in the family of God. We are instructed to go directly to our brother or sister in love. Only if we cannot resolve the issue do we then go to another brother or sister to take back with you. If then for some reason the three of you cannot resolve the issues, then take it to an Elder or Overseer of their ministry.

Saints we have got to get this in our spirits! Division grieves the Holy Spirit so much. satan uses our immaturity and lack of biblical knowledge to keep us disunified. I challenge everyone reading this book to go on a 30 day NO GOSSIP fast.

Before you talk to anyone about anyone else ask yourself-

Is the person I am about to discuss here to defend themselves?

Have I gone one on one in an honest and loving way to give them an opportunity to repent?

Is what I am about to say edify or exhort the person I am about to discuss?

What I am about to say does it harm their reputation or

what the other person might think about them in a negative way?

Have I taken this to prayer first?

If you find out someone has an issue with you then you also need to go one on one and simply ask them. You may find that the people you didn't think you jived with end up being some of your closest friends just by implementing this policy. satan hates a united church. He will come after unity at all costs. Only we can stop it!

I need us to start seeing each other outside of a building. I hear all the time "love your neighbor as yourself" yet I see people who literally live one block from each other that have never even visited each other's homes even though they go to church together. We have become a selfish me-centered church in America. I am sorry if this offends the reader but Saints its true.

For example, I have a single mom in our ministry who really struggled as God took her out of the gutter of life and has planted her into a church and showing Himself to her. She goes to a local church that has many pastors and ministry leaders but not one of them have been to her home. No one has called her to check on her. She has several neighbors that go to the same ministry as her and yet not one has brought her food or even offered to have coffee with her. They have no idea she exists.

Family of God, this is not the biblical Act Chapter 2 of Christianity. My heart ached as she told me her story. She couldn't believe I was in her living room. She couldn't believe I took the time to come see her. All of us have time for coffee. I am a very busy wife, mother, business owner, author, teacher, and mentor but I make time for God's people. Sure, we make time for those who are like us, but do we make time for the single mom, the young man struggling, the elderly, the shut in, the sick, the oppressed?

Family of God, I have met teenagers who tried to commit suicide the night before coming to youth group and no one even noticed them. We have to pay attention to our neighbors. Who is sitting next to you in the pew? Who is across the room? One thing I do every Sunday is before I get to church, I ask God, "Father, show me who needs ministered to today, show me my assignment here today, I am Your hands and feet."

I have never gone to church were there wasn't someone who God illuminated for me to be of service to. Sometimes my assignment is only for that day, other times I need to get with them outside of church.

My final rant is this, Church we have to take holiness seriously. We are looking to much like the world. We watch Rated R movies, we support ungodly institutions that support abortions, sex slave industry and satanic worship, we drink too much, we eat too much, we curse, we dress immodestly, we love money, and the things money can buy in an unhealthy way. I am not here to scold the church, but Saints, Christ is coming back for a bride unspotted by the world. We go into the world to give the good news of the gospel but then we must dust our feet off and use some spot cleaner on the dirt that may have gotten on us while we had the encounters. It's time we stop justifying sin in our lives. Stop justifying watching shows that support sexual immorality, drunkenness, homosexuality, domestic violence. I get that it is not easy, during my early walk I watched things that today I wouldn't fathom watching. I am only asking that you pray and really seek God on what things in your life are you doing that you know Jesus would not do if He was sitting right next to you?

We have to get out lives cleaned up.

Jesus is returning soon and He is developing His end time army.

We need to expect persecution.

We have to stop playing church.

We have to grow up and get unified and start acting like Jesus. We are His ambassadors on earth. We are His hands and feet saints. We have the ministry of

reconciliation. Please saints awake from your slumber. The church has been silent for too long. We have been complacent for too long. We have allowed the enemy to defeat us for too long. Rise up warriors and let's take the kingdom of God by force (in love of course).
Sister Amy

WORKS CITED

*C*harismanews.com "The Reasons for so Many False conversions" by Bert Farias 7/28/2017

Farias, B. (2017, July 28). *The Reasons for so Many False Conversions*. Charisma News | Breaking News. Spiritual Perspective. https://charismanews.com

Got Questions Ministries. (2021, April 26). *What is cultural*

Christianity? GotQuestions.org. https://gotquestions.org

In U.S., decline of Christianity continues at rapid pace. (2020, June 9). Pew Research Center's Religion & Public Life Project. https://www.pewforum.org/2019/10/17/in-u-s-decline-of-christianity-continues-at-rapid-pace/

Myers, J. (2011, December 17). *Is crusade*

evangelism effective? Redeeming God. https://redeeminggod.com/crusade-evangelism-effective/

ABOUT THE AUTHOR

Amy Ross is a teacher at BeTheChurch Ministry. She teaches and councils women of faith to become who God has designed them to be through Christ. Amy has been married to her husband Stephen for 22 years. They have a daughter together and enjoy doing ministry work as a team. Amy is passionate about loving God, loving People and Making Christ known and teaching others to do the same.

Printed in Great Britain
by Amazon

56742503R00076